# Table of Contents

# Sarah's Questions

Sarah couldn't believe her eyes. Her class was on a school trip to a nearby farm. She knew there would be sheep and cows. She was sure she'd see chickens and goats. But a camel?

Farmers Matt and Julie showed the students around. They explained how things worked at the farm. Julie talked about keeping the animals healthy.

# Tell Me Why

# WHY?

# Camels Have Humps

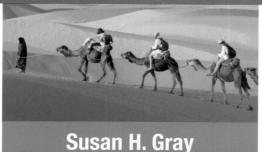

Susan H. Gray

Published in the United States of America by Cherry Lake Publishing
Ann Arbor, Michigan
www.cherrylakepublishing.com

Content Adviser: : Dr. Stephen S. Ditchkoff, Professor of Wildlife Sciences,
Auburn University, Auburn, Alabama
Reading Adviser: Marla Conn, ReadAbility, Inc.

Photo Credits: © PathDoc/Shutterstock Images, cover, 1, 15; © xavier gallego morell/Shutterstock Images,
cover, 1, 9; © michaeljung/Shutterstock Images, cover, 1, 5, back cover; © aleksandr hunta, Shutterstock
Images. cover, 1, 21; © Fred Hendriks/Shutterstock Images, cover, 1, 17; © kyu/Shutterstock Images,
cover, 1, 9; © Kichigin/Shutterstock Images, 5; © lloyd thornton/Shutterstock Images, 7; © John Copland/
Shutterstock Images, 11; © mariakraynova/Shutterstock Images, 13; © Sindre E/Shutterstock Images, 15;
© Konstantnin/Shutterstock Images, 17

Library of Congress Cataloging-in-Publication Data

Gray, Susan Heinrichs, author.
  Camels have humps / by Susan H. Gray.
     pages cm. -- (Tell me why)
  Summary: "Offers answers to their most compelling questions about this
desert-dwelling animal that stores fat in their humps. Age-appropriate
explanations and appealing photos. Additional text features help students
locate information and learn new words"-- Provided by publisher.
  Audience: Grade K to 3.
  Includes bibliographical references and index.
  ISBN 978-1-63188-001-8 (hardcover) -- ISBN 978-1-63188-044-5 (pbk.) --
ISBN 978-1-63188-087-2 (pdf) -- ISBN 978-1-63188-130-5 (ebook)  1.
Camels--Juvenile literature. 2.  Humps (Anatomy)--Juvenile literature. 3.
Children's questions and answers.  I. Title.

QL737.U54G69 2015
599.63'62--dc23

                          2014005725

Cherry Lake Publishing would like to acknowledge the work of The Partnership for 21st Century Skills.
Please visit www.p21.org for more information.

Printed in the United States of America
Corporate Graphics Inc.

**LOOK!**

What features does this camel have that help it survive in a cold area?

*Some camels have two humps and some have one hump.*

Then they came to the camel pen. Sarah's classmates were full of questions. Why does the farm have a camel? What does a camel eat? Does it get along with the other animals?

Sarah waited patiently. Finally, she got to ask her question. "Why does the camel have those humps?" Julie smiled at Sarah's question. People asked that all the time. Julie said that she could answer Sarah. But first she would talk about the camel's natural **habitat**.

*In their natural environment camels sometimes live in groups.*

# Dry Lands

Camels are **mammals**. They have lived in the desert for thousands of years. Deserts are very dry areas. The weather may be hot or cold, but it almost never rains. In cold deserts, snow, sleet, and hail are rare.

When it does rain, the showers do not last long. Puddles, ponds, and little streams might form. But they dry up quickly.

Some deserts are dry and sandy. They may be flat or covered with **dunes**. Such deserts exist in Arabia and northern Africa.

## MAKE A GUESS!

**What if a desert received no moisture at all? Could plants or animals survive there?**

*Camels can be used for transportation.*

Other deserts have rocky ground. They might also be covered with poor soil or small gravel.

Only the toughest plants can grow in the desert. They must be able to survive on very little water. Such plants are built for this hard life. They may not grow very large. Or they might have a waxy skin that reduces water loss to the air.

Camels and cacti can live in the dry desert climate.

Desert animals are also quite hardy. They manage with barely any water. They may have to eat short, **scrubby** plants. In the Sahara Desert of Africa, they face burning hot days. In the Gobi Desert of Asia, they deal with freezing cold winds. Camels survive just fine in these **arid** lands.

*Some camels live in very cold deserts.*

# Built to Survive

The camel is built for life in a desert. Its nose, eyes, lips, and toes are made to deal with this harsh environment. Its hump also helps it survive.

A camel has two large nostrils. When the desert air is calm, the nostrils open wide and the camel breathes freely. But when it's windy, sand and dust swirl about. So the camel clamps its nostrils shut. This keeps dirt out of the animal's lungs.

*Even a camel's nostrils help it survive in the desert.*

Bushy eyebrows and superlong eyelashes shield the eyes. The eyebrows help to shade the eyes on sunny days. The lashes keep out the sand.

Even the animal's lips are made for desert life. Camels feed on plants. But desert plants can be tough and chewy. Many grow close to the ground. The camel's upper lip is adapted for such food. The lip is split down the middle. The left and right sides can move independently. They work together to pluck the plants from the ground.

## ASK QUESTIONS!

Visit a farm or zoo where camels live. Ask a worker what kind of food the camels are fed.

*Camels have adapted to life in the desert.*

The camel's foot has two large toes. They are wide, thick, and very tough. They allow the animal to walk in snow or hot sand without sinking or hurting.

The hump is especially important. A camel stores fat in that hump. The fat is the camel's backup food supply. **Bactrian** camels have two humps. **Dromedary** camels have one hump.

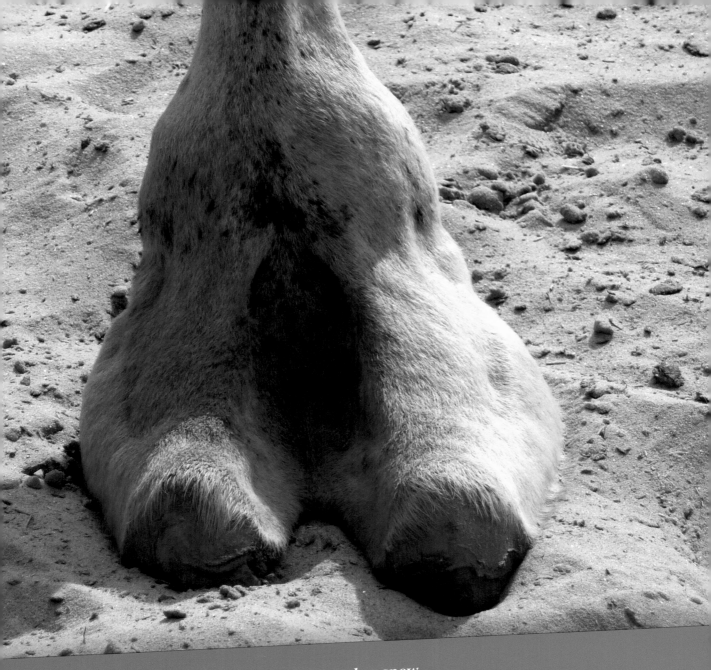

*A camel's wide foot doesn't sink into sand or snow.*

Sometimes, camels cannot find enough food in the desert. So they begin using the fat stored in their humps. The fat provides energy so the camel can keep going. As the fat is used up, the hump shrinks. It gets floppy or slumps over.

When food becomes available, the camel loads up. Its hump grows and straightens up again. It can take one-humped and two-humped camels months to fill up completely. Camels with full humps might be lugging as much as 80 pounds (36 kilograms) of fat!

*This camel does not have fat stored in its humps now.*

# Think About It

Camels living in the Sahara Desert eat prickly cactus to survive. How do you think the camel is able to avoid being harmed by the plant?

What if a camel had no hump? Could it still live in the desert?

Did you know that camels can be used for transportation? Describe how you think it would feel to ride a camel.

# Glossary

**arid** (AR-id) very dry

**Bactrian** (BAK-tree-un) a camel with two humps

**dunes** (DOONZ) hills, mountains, or ridges made of sand

**dromedary** (DRAH-mi-der-ee) a camel with one hump

**habitat** (HAB-i-tat) the natural home of a plant or animal

**mammals** (MAM-uhlz) animals that have hair or fur and usually give birth to live babies

**scrubby** (SKRUHB-ee) small and not growing well

# Find Out More

### Books:

Fisher, Doris. *Army Camels: Texas Ships of the Desert*. Gretna, LA: Pelican Publishing, 2013.

Ganeri, Anita. *I Wonder Why Camels Have Humps and Other Questions About Animals*. New York: MacMillan/Kingfisher, 2003.

Winner, Cherie. *Camels*. Minneapolis: Lerner Publications, 2008.

### Web Sites:

Britannica Kids—Camel
*http://kids.britannica.com/elementary/article-352902/camel*
Watch a video that explains the difference between dromedary camels and Bactrian camels.

National Geographic Kids—Animals: Creature Features
*http://kids.nationalgeographic.com/kids/animals/creaturefeature/camels*
See great photos and read more facts about Bactrian camels.

## Index

## About the Author

Susan H. Gray has a master's degree in zoology. She has worked in research and has taught college-level science classes. Susan has also written more than 140 science and reference books, but especially likes to write about animals. She and her husband, Michael, live in Cabot, Arkansas.